# D is for Drum

## A Native American Alphabet

Written by Debbie and Michael Shoulders and Illustrated by Irving Toddy

Sleeping Bear Press™
2395 South Huron Parkway, Suite 200
Ann Arbor, MI 48104

www.sleepingbearpress.com

Printed and bound in the United States.

20 19 18 17 16 15 14 13

Library of Congress Cataloging-in-Publication Data

Shoulders, Debbie.
D is for drum : a Native American alphabet / written by Debbie and Michael
Shoulders ; illustrated by Irving Toddy.
p. cm.
Summary: "Readers get an A-Z introduction to the customs and cultures of the
first people inhabiting the Americas. Topics include Bison, tipis, Kachinas,
and dugout canoes.—Provided by publisher.
Includes bibliographical references.
ISBN 978-1-58536-274-5
1. Indians of North America—Juvenile literature. 2. Indians of North America—
Social life and customs—Juvenile literature. 3. Alphabet books. I. Shoulders,
Debbie. II. Toddy, Irving, ill. III. Title.
E77.4.S54 2006
970.004'97—dc22                    2005027879

*For my mother, Mary Jane, who gave me my love of reading.*
*For my father, Desmond, who showed me the world.*

DEBBIE

*Special thanks to Aimee Jackson and Irving Toddy for incredible vision.*

MIKE

❧

*I would like to dedicate this book to my wife, Stella, and our children.*

IRVING

# A a

**A** is for Anasazi

The Anasazi, or "ancient ones," lived a thousand years ago. They built elaborate stone and clay buildings in the area known as "the four corners." This is where the four states of Colorado, Utah, Arizona, and New Mexico meet. Called "basket makers," they used tree bark and plant fibers to weave exquisite baskets. The Anasazi civilization flourished until the late 1200s, then mysteriously disappeared from the area. Some historians believe that a drought may have forced the people to move. Modern day Pueblos descended from the Anasazi.

The **A**nasazi were skillful cliff dwellers
but their history remains unclear.
Was it drought, disease, or a mysterious event
that caused them to disappear?

Millions of majestic Bison roamed freely through fields of grass on the plains.
A much-needed resource, they sustained the tribes through their useful life-giving remains.

**B** is for North American Bison

North American Bison is the largest land mammal in North America. While millions of bison used to roam freely across the Great Plains, by the late nineteenth century, European settlers had wiped out most of them, leaving fewer than two hundred animals. Today small bison herds still roam the plains, carefully nurtured and protected by conservation groups.

Native Americans of the plains centered their lives around the bison. Men pursued the animals, sometimes driving them over cliffs or forcing them toward V-shaped pens. Women dried bison meat to create pemmican, a mixture of meat, fat, and berries. A tanned hide became bedding and shelter. Bones were shaped into tools and weapons. Hair was fashioned into such items as bowstrings, ropes, and belts. Boiled fat rendered soap. Even the knuckles of the animal were chewed like modern chewing gum.

Native people no longer hunt the bison, but they still respect the animals by maintaining herds and promoting conservation efforts.

Bb

Natives used dugout Canoes for travel,
and Corn was grown for food.
They used these items almost daily
then gave thanks in gratitude.

**C** is for Corn and Canoe

Native Americans have traditionally used canoes as a method of travel through river systems. They were dug out and carved from the trunks of trees or constructed with bark. They could be up to 25 feet (7.5 meters) long. Native people of Canada used giant red cedars while the Native people of Florida used cypress trees. The bark of the white birch was considered to be the best type of wood for canoes. It was found in Canada and the northeastern United States. Called a "wooden wonder," a canoe of white birch was light enough to be held by one person but strong enough to carry twenty passengers. Modern canoes are constructed from aluminum or fiberglass.

Many Native Americans consider corn, called "maize" by some, the most important grain. The grain is celebrated in Native cultures with festivals at planting and harvest time.

# D is for Drum

Most celebrations of Native cultures include dancing. Native children are taught to dance from an early age. There are many kinds of dances but each has its own name, movements, and history. Many Natives of desert cultures dance and sing during the spring and summer to bring rain. Powwows are another popular type of gathering today where various dances are performed, often for competition.

Drums may be as old as man. Ancient people found wood and gourds to use in ceremonies. People of the Northern Plains stretch animal skins over logs planted in the ground and people of the Southeast pull deerskin over a log to build a water drum. Pacific Coast people use wooden boxes as drums. Many cultures stretch animal skins, like those of bison and elk, over a frame to construct the instrument. Native American drums are thought to "carry the heartbeat of Mother Earth." The pounding of the round drum brings balance to Native people and nation.

Dd

Ceremonies often include dancers dancing
to the beating of a Drum.
The music and movement offer hope
that life-giving rain will come.

**E**

**E**arth lodges seemed to spring from the ground.
They were made from soil, brush, and logs.
They housed members of the tribe, their horses,
their possessions, and even their dogs.

**E** is for Earth lodge

Tipis are often the most depicted dwelling for the bison hunters of the plains. However, some farming communities used the earth to build homes, which were called earth lodges. Dome-shaped and covered with brush as well as sod, the structure could be as large as 55 feet (16.5 meters) in diameter. A lodge of this size would accommodate 40 or more people for ceremonies. Smaller lodges were constructed by piling earth over a wooden frame. These dwellings held the family, including their horses and dogs.

**F** is for Flute

The flute was often used as a courting instrument, played by young men. Flutes are made from many different natural materials depending on what is available in the region. For example, the Choctaw and Cherokee use river cane, while the Sioux, Kiowa, and Zuni carve flutes of white or red cedar and describe the sound of these instruments as the "wind that breathes life into the heart."

Most Native American flutes are constructed with six finger holes, which represent the Earth, the sky, and the four directions: north, south, east, and west. Native flute music continues to be admired and enjoyed.

For a young Native man who was very much in love there really was no substitute. He courted a girl by playing sweet songs to her on his favorite **F**lute.

Ff

The Great Basin of the West was filled
with valuable minerals like **G**old.
Prospectors came, scarred the Earth,
and plundered the resources of old.

**G** is for Gold

Native people hunted and flourished in the Great Basin area of the western United States until the Gold Rush of the 1850s. More and more non-Native people arrived in hopes of getting rich. They eventually stayed and established towns. The newly arrived settlers introduced to the Native people different skills in farming, tending cattle and sheep, crafting jewelry, and building homes. However, many of the Native people were seized as slaves and their land taken. Land that had been rich with deer and rivers abundant with salmon changed as miners hunted the deer and spoiled the rivers with silt.

**H** is for Horse

Modern horses came to North America when the Spanish traded them to the Comanche, beginning in 1541. The Comanche traded the animals to other Native people and the horse became an important part of life on the plains, including bison hunts. Prior to horses, dogs provided help with hunting, so horses were often called "sacred dogs." Horses were valuable to the bison hunter tribes of the plains, and wars were fought for them. Horse races helped Native men with their hunting and fighting skills.

Horses were critical to the hunt.
As wind swept through their mane,
their speed and strength brought much success
to hunters on the plain.

When Europeans first arrived on the shores of a new frontier, six hundred nations of **I**ndigenous people were already living here.

# Ii

**I** is for Indigenous

Native Americans and First Nation refer to the indigenous people of North America. Indigenous groups are Native to a particular region and have kept their distinct languages, characteristics, and culture through time.

There are many scientific theories of how North America was populated. Each Native community has its own explanation of creation, too. The Comanche believe that the Great Spirit gathered swirls of dust from the four directions of the Earth to create its people. The Sioux tell of a Creating Power who makes three worlds. The animals of the first world do not behave correctly so the world is burned. The second world is drowned, but the third world with men who were born of red and white earth see a rainbow. The rainbow signifies that the rain has stopped, allowing human beings and animals to live together in peace. The Inuit, Haida, and Tlingit give credit to Raven who brought light and people to a land of darkness.

With their own legends, languages, and customs, there were more than 600 nations thriving in North America when Europeans arrived during the sixteenth century. Today, more than 500 indigenous nations remain in North America.

Turquoise, silver, and copper are fashioned into objects of striking beauty. Crafting Earth's natural resources into Jewelry is an artisan's skillful duty.

**J** is for Jewelry

Beautiful jewelry is part of the Native American heritage. Coastal communities used shells like abalone to create ear and nose rings with a "mother-of-pearl" finish. Navajo and Hopi fashioned gold, silver, and turquoise into bracelets, rings, chokers, and breastplates. European traders introduced porcelain and glass, which were added to coral, wood, and bone as beadwork for the making of intricate necklaces. Adopting Spanish silversmithing techniques, Navajo and Zuni artists created the characteristic Squash Blossom necklace. Native people of the Southwest continue to be renowned for their silver and turquoise jewelry.

Jj

The words Kachina and Kiva
begin with the letter K.
One guides the prayers of southwestern people.
The other is a place to pray.

**K** is for Kiva and Kachina

From ancient times Pueblo people designed their villages to include an underground chamber called a kiva. Modern kivas can be rectangular or circular with a wooden roof. The men enter a hatchway with a ladder. In the center of the kiva stands a great fire surrounded by pottery filled with sacred herbs. An opening in the floor represents the entrance to the lower world from which all life emerged. Religious ceremonies take place in the smoky kiva.

Spirits known as kachinas have always guided the prayers of the Hopi and Zuni people of the Southwest. It is believed that these spirits descend into special men. The men wear masks, which represent the different spirits, and perform sacred dances that ensure the circle of life. Carved Kachina dolls educate the people about the spirits and are not considered toys.

## L is for Lacrosse

Lacrosse, a sport still popular today, originated from the game of stickball, called Toli, and played by the Choctaw. It helped men prepare for such life skills as hunting and war. Stickball was called "war's little brother." The sport involved up to 100 players on two teams. The players used three-feet (0.9-meter) long wooden sticks that were bent and strung with animal hide. A ball of hide was fashioned and filled with animal hair. There were no boundaries on the playing field and the goal could be 100 feet (30 meters) wide. A team won when they scored 12 goals. With no real rules for fairness, injuries and even deaths were common. Spectators bet on the results of the sport, which was so important to the Choctaw that players drank sacred medicines and performed ritual dances before the match to ensure a positive outcome to the game.

Ll

Lacrosse is the oldest sport in America.
It helped Native people prepare for war.
With hundreds of players and games lasting for days,
it was a challenge for teams to score.

# M m

The healer's **M**edicine pouch carried herbs
and plants for a much-needed cure.
The soft hide bag symbolized hopes and dreams
and helped to reassure.

**M** is for Medicine pouch

The tribal healer often carried a soft hide or beaded bag that contained plants and herbs necessary for calling upon spiritual help in curing illness. Some considered tobacco to be sacred and to have magical powers to heal many ailments, especially snakebite and bee stings. Salicylic acid, extracted from willow trees, worked like aspirin as a painkiller. A tea made from the roots of dandelions was drunk for heartburn. Iris roots mixed with ground suet and beeswax eased abrasions, while the juice of lady's slipper roots, or the inner bark of the Native Hemlock helped with colds and flu. Modern Native American healing traditions still include the use of herbs like sage or skunk cabbage from traditional medicine pouches.

Naming a child is an important tradition in many Native cultures. Often times relatives or elders select the name. The Assateague of the eastern woodlands ask the elder for a name before the child is born because it takes time and prayer to choose a proper name. The naming ceremony for the Nakota of the plains involves time in a sweat lodge as the elders pray for the Creator to watch over the child. The Hopi place two perfect ears of corn on either side of the newborn's head for 19 days. On the 20th day the child's grandmother gives the newborn a name and places a pinch of cornmeal in the baby's mouth, exclaiming, "I wish you a long life and happiness." A feast of cornmeal pudding and hominy stew is given for the entire village to welcome its newest member. The names of most Native nations mean "the people" or "us." When the Europeans arrived they attempted to write down the sounds of the Native language. These words became names of places like Canada, from the Huron-Iroquoian word "kanata," meaning village; Minnesota from the Dakota Sioux word "mnishota," meaning sky-tinted water; or Kentucky, from the Cherokee word meaning land of tomorrow.

Native Names are important words.
They're given to newborns with care.
Honi means wolf, Woya means dove,
and Nita is Choctaw for bear.

**O** is for Osage Orange tree

The Osage carved the wood of the Osage Orange tree to construct bows and arrows. Of medium height, the tree's limbs grow thick and gnarled. This makes them flexible and difficult to break. Crafting a bow involves forty hours of work. Constructing a dozen arrows involves twenty hours of toil. Each piece of wood is carefully examined for its unique properties and then shaped. Today's artisans still follow the tradition of handcrafting bows when using Osage Orange wood.

Bows and arrows are often made
from the limbs of an Osage Orange tree.
It will bend, but is very hard to break.
It's as strong as it can be.

A wooden bowl is elaborately crafted.
It will soon be given away.
It's part of a Potlatch, provided by the host,
and is gratefully put on display.

P p

**P** is for Potlatch

Potlatch is a Chinook word meaning "to give." The potlatch celebrated a wedding, a new totem pole, or a plentiful salmon run. It was also a way to honor the dead or make an action legal, such as acceptance of a new chief. Participants in the celebration sang and danced. The host honored the clan's good fortune and wealth through the presentation of gifts. If the gifts were substantial, the host could raise the honor and status of the clan. Also important to the potlatch was a feast that could last up to twelve days. Guests were treated to such treats as seal meat, fish, and berries.

**Q** is for Quillwork

Native people used porcupine quills to decorate with intricate designs. Patterns of porcupine quills embellished such items as breastplates, quivers (containers for holding arrows), and bow cases. Modern quillworkers can pluck up to 30,000 spiky quills from a single porcupine, following the direction of the hair. The quillworkers soften the quills in water. They color them with natural dyes from berries, flowers, leaves, roots, and bark and then flatten the quills. Sewn into buckskin clothing such as tunics, leggings, and dresses with bison sinew, the quills also provide adornment for cradleboards, women's saddlebags, and household storage articles.

Quillwork provides a social time,
when artisans gather and do their best,
using quills from birds or porcupines,
to decorate moccasins and vests.

# R r

Native Americans make **R**attles from many things:
turtles, gourds, and horns.
The noise is made by adding in pebbles
or dried kernels from an ear of corn.

**R** is for Rattles

After the human voice, the rattle was the next most important musical instrument. The tribal healer also used rattles. They were constructed in many different ways depending on the resources of the area. The Mohawks dried and cleaned a turtle shell, leaving the head, tail, and legs undamaged, and filled it with pebbles. The Creeks loaded a gourd or cattle horn with kernels of corn. The Tlingits carved their rattles out of wood and added human hair to adorn the figure, and the Pueblo people used dried gourds. Traditional Native American music is still enhanced by the sound of cow and turtle shell rattles.

The **S**haman is called when someone is ill
to analyze, pray, and prescribe
which herb or root or special cure
will heal the sick member of the tribe.

S s

Northwestern Native Americans raise Totem poles
from plentiful cedar logs.
The most often carved images are Wolves, Ravens, Bears,
Killer Whales, Thunderbirds, and Frogs.

**Tt**

**T** is for Totem poles

The Native people of the northwest Pacific coast are known for their magnificent carving of totems. Some of the country's largest totem poles can be found in Ketchikan. A trained artist uses cedar trees, a wood with special oils that resists decomposition. Traditionally a totem pole was raised to honor the dead, tell family history and legends, or relate accomplishments. Family stories were usually associated with animals, so the totem pole may include a carving of ravens, wolves, bears, or eagles. Traditional carvers shaped these works of art using tools of stone wedges, yew wood, hammers, and adzes (a curved blade) of chiseled antlers. Dry sharkskin was used to sand the wood and boiled halibut fins provided glue. Today's carvers use power tools and handmade wooden knives, chisels, and adzes to create the structures that give testament to the heritage of the northwestern people.

A wooden frame covered with hides
keeps the Umiak afloat.
It carries people, supplies, and gear
and is called "the women's boat."

## U is for Umiak

The Inuits of the Arctic Ocean have traditionally used an umiak [OO-me-ak] to move their camps in the spring and fall. It was also used for hunting whales. The skin-covered vessel was sometimes called the women's boat because it was usually the women who paddled. The men hunted and fished in kayaks. Traditionally made from two female walrus hides, the umiak was painted white to blend in with the snow-colored background of the North. Seal or walrus skin made the vessel light and the flat bottom held the boat level when pulled up to shore. Designed to be 16 to 40 feet (4.8 to 12 meters) long, it was wider and deeper than a kayak with no decking. Modern umiaks are constructed of fiberglass cloth saturated with a waterproof coating, which provides a light, flexible craft for maneuvering in the waters of the Pacific Northwest.

U u

**V**

Native people might take a journey with the purpose to connect to a spirit during a **V**ision quest. It's a special time to reflect.

**V** is for Vision quest

Traditionally in some Native American cultures, young men have to pass a rite of passage called a vision (or spirit) quest, which can help them to find a guardian spirit. It is a time of fasting and praying. Prior to the journey, the men bathe in a cold stream to overcome fear in preparation for a long stay in the wilderness. They spend time praying and fasting, awaiting the arrival of the spirit.

Either through a dream or an actual visit from an animal such as a bison, bear, wolf, or eagle, each young man saw the spirit that would guide his life. For example, a bison vision might symbolize power and abundance, or a vision of a butterfly might mean the need to change one's life.

This spiritual journey is still important to Native Americans who desire a life-changing experience and a better understanding of the nature of the universe.

Navajo **W**eavers paint like artists.
It takes time, but they do transform
colorful yarn into beautiful blankets
to keep Navajo children warm.

## W is for Weaving

The intricate art of weaving comes predominately from the Navajo people of the Southwest. Early Pueblo people cultivated cotton. The skill was passed on to the Navajo. Spaniards introduced sheep, whose wool is the basis of Navajo weaving. The wool is colored in mixtures of vegetable dyes and charcoal. Navajo women believe that they are taught to weave by the spirit, "Spider Woman." The talent is then passed down to their daughters, along with their weaving tools. Parents might rub spiderwebs on their daughters' hands in hope that they would inherit the ability to weave. Designs are one of a kind and created to denote motion. A skilled weaver can make a blanket in eight to ten weeks, and authentic Native American weavings continue to be valued worldwide.

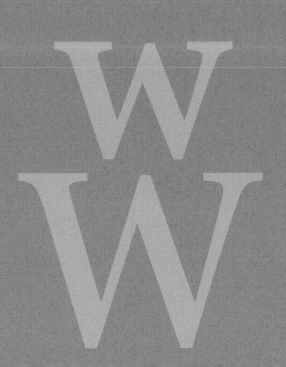

A tribe living on the northwest coast
has a name you must say twice.
They share the land with the white Spirit Bear
and are called by the name Xai Xais.

The Xai Xais [HI-hize] nation is one of 500 indigenous nations of North America that continues to prosper in modern times. Located in Klemtu, a small village on Swindle Island (Kynoc Inlet), British Columbia, the Xai Xais live with the Kitasoo Tribe as residents within the permanent territories of the First Nation. The First Nation refers to the people who first inhabited Canada. The community's population averages about 460 people. Traditionally the Xai Xais have earned a living through commercial fishing. In addition to salmon farming, the people also devote their energies to tourism and forestry, helping to protect the natural beauty of the region, especially the Kermode White Bear, called the "Spirit Bear."

X
X

Yup'ik masks may be relatively small
or so large they are difficult to wear.
Yup'ik dancers depict Artic life
like walrus, fish, berries, and bear.

Y y

**Y** is for Yup'ik masks

The Yup'ik [YOOP-ik], members of the Inuit nation who live in the Arctic region, carve masks that are used as stage props for performances or storytelling rather than being recognized as sacred items. The Yup'ik name comes from "yuk" meaning person and "pik" meaning real. The "real people" present stories with a vast array of experiences, therefore masks are carved to depict animals, insects, berries, wood, and ice. Yup'ik masks are distinctive with their toothy mouths, thumbless hands, goggled eyes, and feather halos. Expert Yup'ik carvers design the masks, each with a distinct style. They can be found in museums dedicated to Native American art.

**Z** is for Zuni pottery.

Pottery is an art form distinctive to Native Americans with natural clay resources. Many Native cultures are known for their pottery. Zuni pottery is especially known for its balanced geometric designs. Using only their hands, Zuni potters work from a base of clay forming distinctive tri-colored bowls and other storage containers with elaborate patterns. Shaped with tools made of dried squashes and painted with yucca plant leaf brushes, the pottery is dipped into a paste of minerals and water. Firing is accomplished by burying the bowls in a mound of hot, dried animal dung or a modern electric kiln. A number of talented craftsmen continue the ancient tradition, creating pieces of fine art.

Talk of beautiful Native art
certainly must include
Zuni pottery, which is used
for meals and serving food.

## Debbie & Michael Shoulders

*D is for Drum: A Native American Alphabet* is Michael Shoulders' sixth book with Sleeping Bear Press and was co-written with his wife Debbie. Michael travels extensively, visiting schools and spreading the word that "reading is magic." Debbie is an educator and writes a weekly column highlighting new children's books. Debbie and Michael live in Clarksville, Tennessee, and are the parents of three children and one very large standard poodle.

## Irving Toddy

Irving Toddy lives with his wife and six children in Pine Springs, Arizona. He is the oldest son of famed Navajo painter, Beatien Yazz. Irving graduated from Utah State University, where he studied painting and illustration. His work is held in collections by both private and institutional collectors, and sold in galleries across the Southwest. He has also illustrated numerous children's books, book covers, and articles for children's magazines. Irving was awarded the "Best in Show" prize at the 64th Inter-Tribal Indian Ceremonial in Gallup, New Mexico.